Slugs

by Kris Bonnell

Slugs do not like the sun.
On sunny days, slugs hide under rocks and logs.
Slugs come out at night and on wet days.

3

A slug has four feelers.
The top two feelers are like eyes.
The top feelers can tell
if it is light or not.
The bottom two feelers
are like a nose.
The bottom feelers can smell.

5

The hole on the side of a slug is also like a nose.
The slug gets air from this hole.

7

The bottom of a slug
is called the foot.
A slug uses its foot to move.
Slugs do not move fast.

9

A slug's mouth is on its foot.

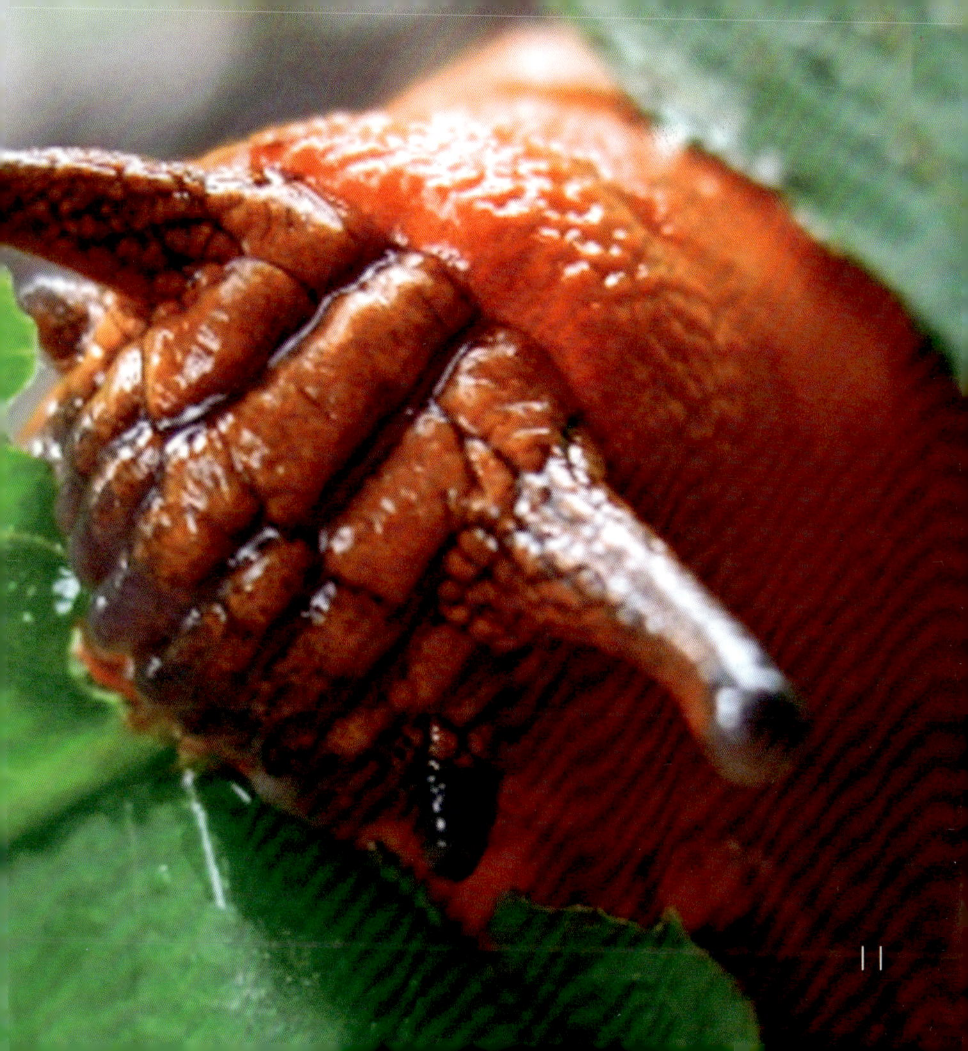

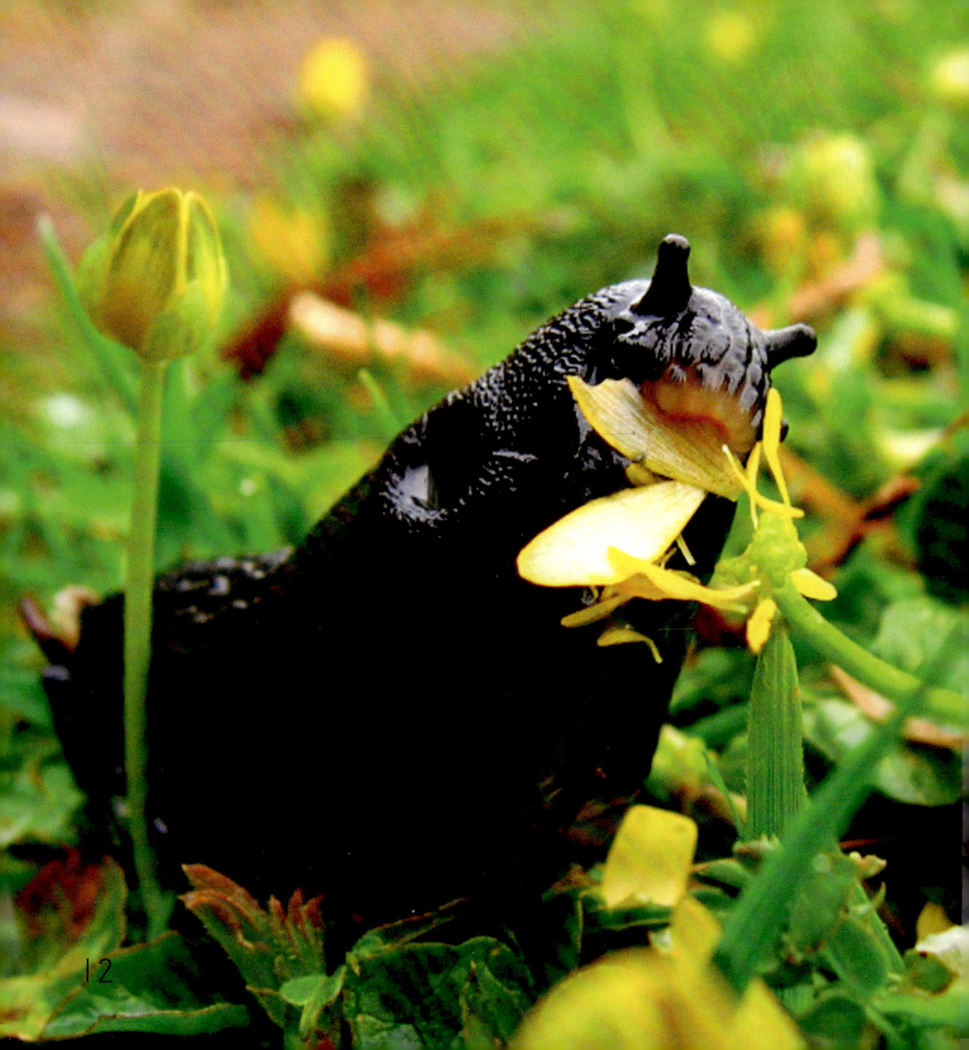

Slugs eat lots of things.

Slugs eat leaves and flowers.

Slugs eat mushrooms.

Some slugs eat worms!

Slugs make slime.

Slime keeps slugs wet.

It also helps slugs move.

Slime helps slugs move upside down.